LIGHT ON
AUSTRALIA

A Portrait of the Australian Landscape

LIGHT ON
AUSTRALIA

A PORTRAIT OF THE AUSTRALIAN LANDSCAPE
BARRY SLADE

Angus&Robertson
An imprint of HarperCollinsPublishers

Previous page: **South Australia's Painted Desert.**

Contents pages (clockwise from top left): **The Pinnacles, Western Australia.**
A weatherbeaten homestead near Omeo, Victoria.
Silverton, New South Wales.
Eucalyptus forest debris, Katherine, Northern Territory.
The Cathedral, Mt Buffalo National Park, Victoria.
Freshwater pool, Cape le Grand National Park, Western Australia.
Creek pebbles, Kalamina Gorge, Hamersley Range, Western Australia.
A dragon lizard (*Ctenophorus caudicinctus*) stakes out its territory in King's Canyon, Northern Territory.

An Angus & Robertson Publication

Angus & Robertson, an imprint of
HarperCollins*Publishers*
25 Ryde Road, Pymble, Sydney NSW 2073, Australia
31 View Road, Glenfield, Auckland 10, New Zealand
77-85 Fulham Palace Road, London W6 8JB, United Kingdom
10 East 53rd Street, New York NY 10022, USA

First published in Australia in 1993

National Library of Australia
Cataloguing-in-Publication data:

Slade, Barry, 1956—
  Light on Australia.
  ISBN 0 207 17483 0.

  1. Landscape — Australia. 2. Landscape — Australia — Pictorial works.
  I. Title.

919.40463

Printed in Hong Kong.

9 8 7 6 5 4 3 2 1
96 95 94 93

ACKNOWLEDGMENTS

I would like to thank National Park staff throughout Australia who were always ready with information and assistance. Thanks are also due to the station owners who assisted me in my photography and more than once helped fix shredded tyres on my four wheel drive; the people on the road who frequently invited me to join their campfires; and finally I thank Pam for looking after the office in my absence.

Central Station, Sydney.

INTRODUCTION

The light which shines on the diverse Australian landscape is reckoned to differ from that found in other parts of the world. It is a clear, hard, direct light which is at its strongest in the torrid outback; but its probing radiance can, at times, illuminate all corners of the continent. Away from the inland, it is often modified, tamed by the local conditions — it may be filtered by forest trees, shadowed by ranges, subdued by the coast's salt-drenched air or lost in the mist and clouds of valleys and highlands. Whatever the topography or climate, however, light remains a shaping force in the Australian environment and, together with the sense of space and of age, helps create the distinctive mood and character of the landscape.

The Australian landscape has experienced great change — it has seen the advance and retreat of continent-spanning forests, inundation by the sea and vast inland lakes, the erosion of mountains and ranges to gentle hills and the tremendous thrusting upwards of plateaus to replace them. Time and change have left their imprint on the environment in ways both subtle and dramatic, and have given Australia its timeworn character.

The present state of this ongoing evolution is a land of great physical and environmental diversity. Arid lands cover more than half of the continent and are home to some of the earth's most impressive landforms. Far from a sterile region of rock and sand, the arid zone is colonised by well-adapted plants and animals. Harboured in these regions are oases of permanent water and ancient, fragile plant colonies; tangible reminders of other epochs.

Bounded by a seemingly limitless coastline of precipitous cliffs, arcing beaches, dunes, headlands, salt flats and mangrove forests, Australia is unique as an island continent. This meeting place of land, sea and sky is a dynamic environment in which spectacle cohabits with tenacious lifeform.

Severity of environment has also shaped the high- lands of the continent's south-east. Freezing temperatures, snow, wild winds and exposed, often treeless surrounds create uncompromising landscapes.

In Australia's great forests, the environment is largely self-creating. Sunshine and rain are collected by the forest canopy, while another rain of leaves and bark feed the soil of the forest floor. The efficiency of this self-sustaining ecology is exemplified in the soaring eucalypt forests of the south-east and south-west of the continent, and finds its most complex expression in an array of superb rainforests.

Above: 'The Lost City' plateau, King's Canyon, Northern Territory.

Left: Spinifex Pigeon, Hamersley Range, Western Australia.

Opposite: A temporary lake, South Australia.

While Australia's natural heritage defies superlatives, much of the land has been changed since European settlement. Rangelands were converted to grazing properties, the plains fenced, planted and grazed, and towns, both short-lived and enduring, sprung up throughout. Apart from the economic benefits of this development, we have been left with a cultural heritage of architecture and lifestyle that continues to enrich the experience of the countryside.

The ecology and topography of Australia's diverse range of environments, the nature of the light which falls upon these

regions, and the way both, in merging, express fundamental qualities of the landscape, are the themes I have attempted to explore in this book. In Australia, the artistry of light and landscape form a potent combination.

DARWIN

Windjana Gorge

Kimberley Region

Bungle Bungle Ranges

Halls Creek

NORTHER

Hamersley Range National Park

Cape Range National Park

Kings Canyon

Ningaloo

Uluru National Pa

Ayers Rock

The Olgas

WESTERN AUSTRALIA

Shark Bay

SOUT

Kalbarri National Park

The Pinnacles

PERTH

Cape le Grand National Park

East Mount Barren

Stirling Ranges

Fitzgerald River National Park

Albany

Cape Leeuwin

Shannon National Park

Torndirrup National Park

Cape York

Abner Range

RITORY

l's Pebbles

• LAWN HILL NATIONAL PARK

• MOUNT SPEC NATIONAL PARK

ce Springs

mbow Valley

'hamber's Pillar

EUNGELLA NATIONAL PARK

Simpson Desert

Longreach •

QUEENSLAND

Carnarvon Gorge

Painted Desert

TRALIA

BUNYA MOUNTAINS NATIONAL PARK •

• BRISBANE

Arkaroola

NEW SOUTH WALES

• GIRRAWEEN NATIONAL PARK

Beltana

• Mootwingee

BALD ROCK NATIONAL PARK

Broken

Hawker •   Hill

• Wilcannia

• CATHEDRAL ROCK NATIONAL PARK

• Quorn

Nyngan •

• HAT HEAD NATIONAL PARK

Silverton

Great Dividing Range

• BARRINGTON TOPS NATIONAL PARK

Hill End • Sofala

• BOUDDI NATIONAL PARK

Murray

Kanangra–Boyd Region

• KU-RING-GAI NATIONAL PARK

ADELAIDE

River

Blue Mountains

SYDNEY

Illawarra Region

—— BOTANY BAY NATIONAL PARK

Coorong Lake

MORTON NATIONAL PARK

VICTORIA

Tumut •   CANBERRA

ounghusband Peninsula

• Dimboola

Lake Bolac

KOSCIUSKO NATIONAL PARK

• Horsham

• MIMOSA ROCKS NATIONAL PARK

The Grampians

Cobungra

Tantawangalo Forest

MELBOURNE •

• Bendoc

Port Campbell

Twelve
Apostles

East
Gippsland

Errinundra Forest

MOUNT BUFFALO NATIONAL PARK

TASMANIA

HOBART •

ARID
LANDS

THE ARID LANDS
STRETCHING ACROSS
AUSTRALIA'S INTERIOR HAVE
POWER AND MYSTIQUE IN THEIR VASTNESS

AND THEIR AGE. IN THESE ANCIENT LANDS THE EROSIVE factors of wind, water, temperature and time have combined to produce jagged and uncompromising landforms. The massive geological formations of Ayers Rock and the Olgas in the Northern Territory, and the Bungle Bungle Ranges in Western Australia have smaller scale counterparts throughout the arid region.

These are lands of extremes and powerful, yet stark, beauty. Exposed rocks on buttes and mesas fracture under ceaseless heating and cooling action, and their debris adds to the slopes of loose rubble. Stoney plains reddened by iron oxide are polished by wind-blown sand, and form glittering expanses dotted randomly by hardy shrubs of bluebush or saltbush. Nothing moves here but the sun, shadows and perhaps a stoic gibberbird.

Vast areas are dominated by sand dunes, thinly vegetated with shrubs and grasses in colours that both complement and contrast with the oxide-coated sand grains. Sound is muted by the sand, leaving only the wind's quiet rush. Occasionally fiercer winds blow. Stinging grains blur the horizon and animal tracks disappear as the landscape re-creates itself. The wind forms ripples of sand which flow grain by grain before the prevailing wind, in time advancing the entire dune.

Dominating the region are the geological masterpieces of Ayers Rock, the Olgas and the Bungle Bungle Ranges which have a scale that the eyes register but at which the imagination falters. The two former, in Uluru National Park, are 600 million year old sedimentary rocks that were uncovered 200 million years ago. That

Left: **The dramatic white trunks of snappy gums are dotted among tussocks of porcupine grass on the gorges of the Hamersley Range, Western Ausralia.**

Previous page: **Devil's Pebbles, Northern Territory.**

3

the entire surrounding region was eroded away to expose the monolithic formations speaks of their majestic antiquity more clearly than any bald number.

The domes of the Bungle Bungle Ranges are like a geological fantasy. Composed of sandstone somewhat younger than the Uluru wonders, their forms flow wave-like across the landscape in a way that suggests they are composed of material more malleable than rock. The suggestion has a trace of validity — beneath the domes' silica capping the sandstone is relatively soft.

Rainbow Valley National Park, Northern Territory.

The often harsh, desolate appearance of the arid lands gives an impression of timelessness — a sense that these lands have remained unchanged for hundreds of thousands of years. While the main cause of aridity was Australia's drift northwards into warmer latitudes beginning about 40 million years ago, there have been many periods since that time in which the climate was relatively benign in inland Australia. The region reached its driest point 20 000 years ago during the last ice age, when rainfall was only half modern averages. Plants retreated to refuges in gorges and creek beds, and many animals became extinct. With the loss of vegetation cover, winds built alluvial material up into dunes and sand plains. As the climate improved from about 12 000 years ago the landscape was reclaimed by vegetation to create the form familiar today.

A massive stone arch frames a distant view of Chamber's Pillar in the Northern Territory. Composed of sandstone more than 350 million years old, the buttes are the remnants of an ancient plateau that has since been eroded to the level of the surrounding plain. Only a capping of iron-rich sandstone has preserved these outcrops.

Sunshine is still so abundant that plants and animals possess mechanisms for protection from its drying heat and radiation. Many trees shed their leaves after prolonged dry spells, waiting in a near dormant state for the next adequate rain. Grasses have tough outer sheaths, which reduce moisture loss, and needle tips to make would-be grazers think twice. Despite all these protective adaptations, the harshness of the environment is revealed by the stunted, twisted form of many trees and shrubs. In sheltered gorges with plenty of moisture, these plants achieve their full growth potential.

Triodia and *Plectrachne* species, native to Australia, are two of the most interesting and important arid region plants. Also known as porcupine grass, a widespread species, *Triodia basedowii*, dies off in the centre of its hummock. Around this dead centre (which may reach a

7

Sandstone cliffs at Rainbow Valley in the Northern Territory. The sandstone is coloured red by iron deposits. On the cliff top, a native cyprus pine survives in the exposed position through its deeply probing roots which extract water from the stone.

diameter of many metres (yards)) a ring of living grass grows shielding the interior from wind and reducing sun exposure.

The dead leaves thus decay in a moister environment where grubs and insects can feed. Native mice, small marsupials and lizards in turn prey on the insects, while larger predators such as birds of prey and dingoes exploit these small creatures. Kangaroos are also known to sleep within the ring of grass, utilising the protection it offers.

For the most part animals take shelter from the sun, spending the day in burrows or rock overhangs and caves. At dawn and during the night they emerge to hunt or graze. Some marsupials don't need to drink at all, gaining moisture from their food. The euros or wallaroo (a type of kangaroo) has been record-ed as not drinking for up to three months, with a porcupine grass diet providing the animal's moisture needs. Large kangaroos rely on nomadic behaviour to avoid very dry conditions. Reptiles, apart from an amount of deliberate sun exposure needed to 'rev them up' for the day, also avoid the sun as much as possible.

Above: **The well-armoured thorny devil searches the hot desert ground for ants. Its spines, as well as providing protection, are also an efficient means of trapping dew which drains into the mouth through capillary action.**

Previous page: **Standing free of the 250 metre (820 feet) cliffs of the western wall of the Bungle Bungles is a massive, pyramid-shaped rock. This outlier is composed of rock more resistant to erosion than that which once linked it to the main wall.**

Above: The fruit of the kapok tree provides a feast for this red-winged parrot.

Below left: Shy wallabies in Cape Range National Park, Western Australia, emerge to graze in the cool of late afternoon.

Following page: The limestone walls of the Windjana Gorge in Western Australia rise above eucalypt and baobabs. The limestone was formed as a barrier reef under the sea 350 million years ago.

Despite the strength with which the sun beats down on these parched landscapes during the day, its heat is just as quick to disappear at night back into the cloudless skies. During winter the temperature drops below zero (32 degrees Fahrenheit) regularly. If there is moisture in the air, frost will form on the ground. This water source is sought out by small opportunistic animals who

Left: **The Bungle Bungle Ranges. Vegetation at the foot of the formations benefits from the water run-off and lower rate of evaporation in these more protected areas.**

Right: **Dark clouds often build up over the arid regions, but their promise of rain is rarely fulfilled. These shrublands are north of Broken Hill in New South Wales.**

perhaps weary of their relatively dry diet. Chilled reptiles lie almost dormant until the morning sun warms the air sufficiently for them to make their way to a sunny spot.

The arid lands can be places of illusion. A river's dry sand bed

Left: An aerial view of the Bungle Bungles. Picaninny Creek winds an often dry course through the rocky formations.

Right: Under the searing heat and rapid cooling of the desert region, rocks eventually fracture and split apart.

Left: Fallen native fuchsia flowers form a decorative pattern on the ground.

mimics in its contours the boil and flow of a stream in flood, while debris, deposited from a flood perhaps years earlier, remains bent and twisted as if resisting the invisible flow. Under the sand, water filters through the grains in an ironic trickle. The tantalising illusion of lakes glimmering on the horizon has truth only in the bitter salt lakes whose expanses are fed from huge desert catchments. But even they eventually dry up, to be replaced by their ghostly image. Distances and scale are also deceptive. The vastness of the landscape tends to downplay the real size of landforms until they are approached more closely.

Rain is a capricious visitor. Often clouds will build up, marching in great massed bands across the sky, only to dissolve away later in the day. Mists of rain will sometimes fall, trailing in the wake of the darker

Above: Sunset, Ayers Rock.

Right: The Devil's Pebbles, Northern Territory, are raked with light from the rising sun.

clouds, randomly soaking red dunes and claypans and attracting birds to temporary pools.

Sometimes rain teems down until the thirsty ground can absorb no more, and the ancient watercourses spread the surplus over the landscape. When this subsides many plants respond to the temporary plentiful supply with a furiously quick reproductive cycle. Flowers burst open, their scent and bright colours competing for the visits of pollen-spreading birds and insects. Seeds form, and are spread by the wind — some rise up on fluffy pods, while other plants roll before the wind, scattering seeds as

Above: Gums are etched out against the gloom of Hancock Gorge, Hamersley Range.

Right: Hardy shrubs struggle for purchase on the loose slopes of the Painted Desert's buttes.

they go. Burrs seek living transport, attaching to fur, hide and, more recently, socks.

Light falls in full measure on the arid lands, flooding the land in the absence of water. It draws lines of shadow sharp and clear across angular rocks, probing briefly into gorges, chasms and caves, and for most of the day contributes to the flatness of the landscape. A high sun mutes with its glare the colours of the outback, and it is not until it nears the horizon that true colour and detail are revealed. The heat absorbed by the rocks during the day then seems to radiate forth as colour, as yellow and red oxides glow in the low sunlight. The texture of acacias and mulgas is picked out and cast into relief by shadow. Rounded clumps of porcupine grass briefly flare up with light.

It is during these brief times that the sun takes on a benign aspect and its unrelenting force during the middle hours of the day is lessened. But mostly the outback light is a searching, glaring light, a hammer light, and all of the arid lands bend to its indifferent will.

Following page:
***Livistonia* palms growing in Echidna Chasm. These palms are native to the Bungle Bungle Ranges and thrive beside sheltered cliffs where they can take advantage of water run-off and percolation.**

OASES

FOUND WITHIN THE ARID LANDS ARE PLACES DRAMATICALLY DIFFERENT TO THE SURROUNDING

ENVIRONMENT. IN THESE CHASMS AND GORGES WATER IS permanently available, and plants and animals survive within protected niches perhaps only 100 metres (yards) from an environment that would prove fatal to them. Shielded by walls of stone, with pools like moats protecting them from the arid invader, these oases are time capsules that provide a glimpse of the ancient history of the Australian continent, when the inland was more fertile than it is today.

Landforms in these areas are invariably striking. Rocks balance on fissures which thread deep into the geological structure; rock sheaths split from the main wall of the gorge and lean precariously over the depths. The effect is of an earthquake arrested at the peak of its mayhem. While everything rests in a temporary truce with gravity, the potential for sudden catastrophe creates a subdued tension in the landscape.

As creeks and rivers perform the unimaginably patient task of gouging out these chasms and gorges, they also reveal geological time as rock strata is uncovered. Silica-rich rocks such as those found in the Hamersley Range in Western Australia, are polished by the gentle, but prolonged action of water. Their surface becomes slick and reflective, and cool to the touch. A sensuous fluidity is passed on from water to stone.

However, under the same force, sandstone retains a more or less abrasive quality. The walls of sandstone gorges split along joint lines, so that great slabs may suddenly give way, to slide

thunderously to the bottom. Left behind are relatively smooth expanses of stone that are impressive in their starkness. Creeks are strewn with boulders broken down from the fallen sheaths of rock and rounded by the action of the water.

Rock, rather than sky, is the dominant element in this environment. The sun is a brief visitor to the depths of the gorges, and temperatures do not alter as much as in exposed areas. These regions are also kept cooler by pools of ice cold water — the sun does not reach them long enough to warm the water, if it strikes them at all. But enough direct and reflected light probes into the caverns and more open gorges to foster the growth of ferns, palms, mosses and cycads where sufficient soil and moisture is present.

Water constantly percolates out of the rock massif, which acts as a slow-release sponge. The water comes from rainfall that has filtered underground. Water percolation and indirect light can lead to the growth of spongy walls of mosses, ferns, lichen and liverworts, which thrive in the constant dripping. At secret pools

Left: **The rare cycad, *Macrozamia macdonnelli*, is found in only a few locations in central Australia. This grove is at King's Canyon, Northern Territory.**

Right: **Joffre Gorge is a deep, winding fracture in the iron-stained rock of the Hamersley Range. The narrowness of the gorge turns it into a channel of tumultous water in heavy rain.**

Previous page: **Reflections from sunlit rocks above turn a shallow stream in Hancock Gorge, Hamersley Range, into a flow of molten gold.**

rare species of fig, tree ferns, palms and cycads arch towards their brief ration of sunlight. In more exposed watercourses casuarinas, acacias and rushes line the banks among taller eucalypts with flood-bared roots.

Floods are, in fact, the greatest environmental hazard gorge inhabitants must face. As these places are natural watercourses, and

Right: Fortescue Falls in the Hamersley Range.

Left: A colony of tree ferns survives on reflected light at the base of the Amphitheatre in Carnarvon Gorge, Queensland. Carved out by water, the walls of the Amphitheatre belly outwards from a narrow opening at the top.

the deepest part of the catchment, floods are likely to be violent. Tree limbs, logs, tumbling stones and other debris race along in the current. Flexible plants, such as reeds and ferns, prove most resilient to the force of the flood.

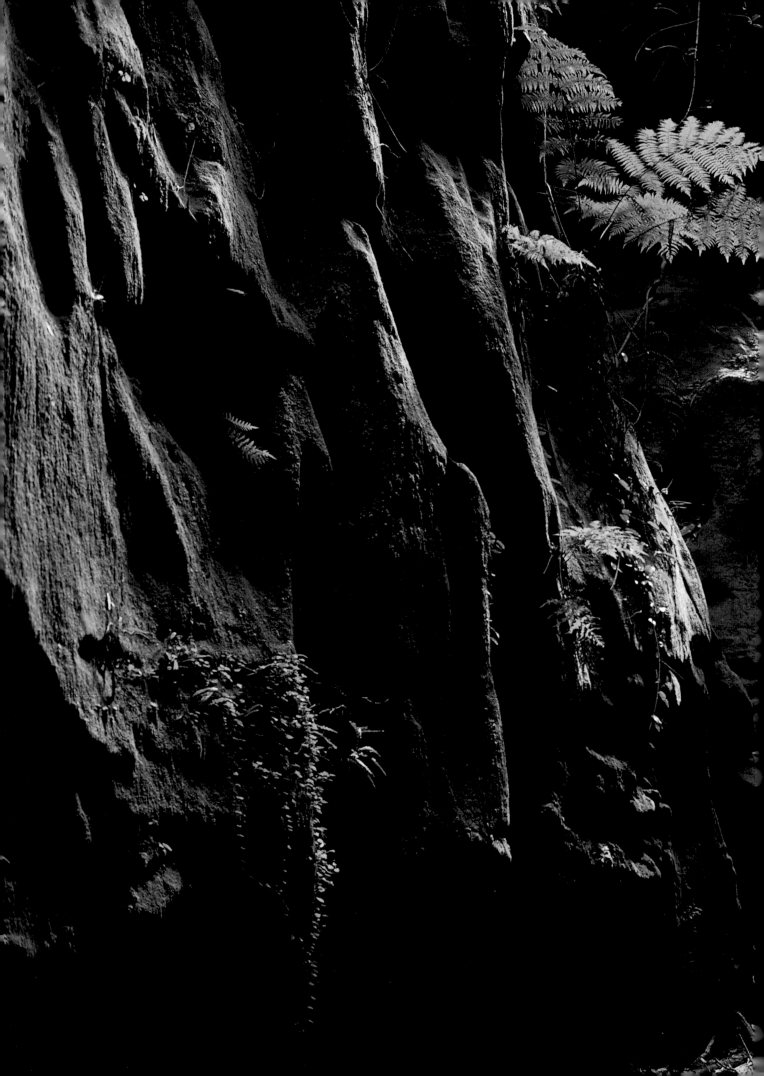

In other ways floods can be beneficial. Creekside vegetation, after long periods of stability, may become choked with vines and creepers such as the native passionfruit, and only a vigorous flood will sweep the vine away. In addition, nutrient-rich soil and plant matter from the surrounding plateaus are swept into the gorges, to settle as the current eases, providing a stimulus for new vegetation.

The world of the gorges is, by definition, largely enclosed. This causes changes in the way things are perceived within them. Sounds are magnified and directed by the enclosing walls so that they carry further. A moving stone echoes from wall to wall, a trickling waterfall is two bends distant, and a rock pigeon taking flight 200 metres (yards) away will sound as if it has taken flight beside you.

While the air is mainly still and cool, sudden breezes can arise as the rocks overhead heat in the sun and temperature differentials occur. Narrow passages, where insects are likely to be swept through on the breeze, are the favoured positions for spiders

Previous page: **Ward's Canyon in Carnarvon Gorge harbours one of Australia's rarest and most primitive plants — the king fern *Angiopterus evicta*. The fern's vascular structure is quite unlike that found in modern plants.**

Left: **Well-watered and sheltered by the enclosing walls of Frog Pond Gorge in the Bungle Bungle Ranges, a colony of *Livistonia* palms thrives. Isolated from relatives in other parts of Australia many thousands of years ago by aridity, these palms have evolved into a separate species.**

Right: **Fig trees maintain a tenacious hold on the magnificently sculptured sandstone spires and domes of the Abner Range in the Northern Territory.**

Above: A flying buttress formation, Abner Range.

Left: A permanent pool of water in Cathedral Chasm reflects the rock formations of the Bungle Bungle Ranges.
Trees and shrubs thrive next to the permanent source of water, although direct sunlight is strictly rationed.

to construct their webs. They will sit patiently in the web, or rock back and forth as if testing the strength of their constructions.

Colours are generally muted in the darker surrounds and are influenced by reflection from the blue sky. When the sun does

Right: St Andrew's Cross spiders weave their webs in narrow parts of gorges, catching insects blown off course by fluke winds.

Left: A stream races along its rocky bed in Hancock Gorge. These iron and silica-rich rocks, cool and smooth to the touch, originated as sediment on the sea floor two and a half billion years ago.

briefly probe into the canyon depths, the actual colours are dramatically revealed, in the same way an underwater camera flash will reveal the true colour of coral.

Quiet pools in the depths of gorges and chasms are fertile places for surprises, and for discoveries of light, shape and colour. Reflections from still pools repeat the shapes above, creating an

illusion of depth in the shallow water. Sunlight reflecting from a pool disturbed by a thrown pebble will cast spreading concentric circles of light, in perfect form, onto an overhanging rock ledge. Sunlight shafts into the green water, where fish and frogs are briefly revealed, before they again disappear into blackness. Like a narrow searchlight, the beam slowly creeps across the pool, gradually contracting as the sun is cut off by the overhanging crevasse. At length only reflected light is left, and this becomes more and more subdued as afternoon merges into evening.

Apart from harbouring unique plant and animal species, some of which are found nowhere else on the continent, the dramatic contrast of these oases with their arid surrounds, the context in which they are found and the suddenness of the transition, make them special and rare places to be cherished and protected.

Right: Leichhardt trees lining Lawn Hill Creek, north west Queensland. The cluster figs, cabbage palms and fern varieties found in this forest are the remnants of rainforest that covered this now predominantly arid region some 15 million years ago.

Left: Blue water lilies, Lawn Hill Creek.

Following page: A southerly change brings with it driving wind and rain, buffetting the sandstone cliffs of the Royal National Park, south of Sydney.

THE COAST

AS AN ISLAND
CONTINENT, AUSTRALIA'S
COASTAL ENVIRONMENT

EMBRACES A WIDE RANGE OF GEOLOGICAL STRUCTURES AND TERRAIN. WITH MORE THAN 30 000 kilometres (18 630 miles) of coastline, the constant theme is the convergence of the primary elements of land, sea and sky. This convergence creates a wealth of atmosphere, life, drama and subtlety in these regions.

Some coastlines are ill-defined — in these regions, the surrounding terrain is generally level, almost flush with the sea, and the transition from land to sea is a long gradual affair. Sediment is regularly deposited by river run-off. In mangrove communities, the sea channels wander leisurely, not so much flowing, as rising and falling with the tide.

Few plant species can survive here without special adaptations. Mangroves have salt-excreting pores on their leaves and some species have roots that probe into the air for their gas interchange. For the creatures which inhabit these areas, mangroves provide an environment as rich as a rainforest. The constant rain of dead leaves combines with decaying sea-grass and other sediments to produce fertile conditions for micro-organisms. Shellfish, crabs and juvenile fish feed on these and in turn become prey for successively larger creatures.

In contrast to the salt flats and low muddy islands of the mangrove communities, the boundary between land and sea in some places could not be more abrupt. Imposing cliff faces front the oceans in uncompromising ranks, waves battering ceaselessly at their bases. This is a form of slow water torture where individual waves are powerless, but their combined effect over hundreds of

The root stems of mangroves thrust into the air on this Shark Bay shoreline, Western Australia.

years results in the cliffs eventually crumbling into the sea. The relationship between land and sea is an adversarial one.

The way in which cliffs erode depends on their geological origin and structure. Sandstone tends to be relatively stable for long periods until undercutting and atmospheric weathering cause great slabs to sheer off in sudden avalanches. Harder igneous rocks (formed deep underground and subject to heat and pressure) are more resistant to erosive pressures. Some areas of coast feature exposed basalt columns, which look as if they were constructed, fortress-like, to resist the sea's battery. Limestone, which originates from calcite deposits of corals and shellfish, forms cliffs that can be the most treacherous underfoot. Sea and rain dissolves the limestone, resulting in a relatively swift change in the rock's exterior. Caves are hollowed out at the cliff base and crumbling surfaces form elsewhere. Shale is another rock form which offers less resistance to the erosive forces of the coastal environment.

A massive natural bridge of granite spans a chasm near Albany in Torndirrup National Park, Western Australia.

Beaches are the pulverised remains of the seemingly indomitable cliffs, and they form some of Australia's most spacious landscapes. The ocean beaches define great lengths of the coastline, sometimes extending in stretches of well over 100 kilometres (over 60 miles). These vast beaches extend beyond vision, disappearing into a haze of pale sand, salt spray and foaming swells.

Tannin from heath vegetation stains this creek brown, as it makes its way to Thistle Cove in Cape le Grand National Park, Western Australia.

Although they are constantly being re-created in innumerable subtle ways, beaches retain a relative uniformity of appearance. Only the great storms that pound the beaches from time to time, gouging out sand and dumping it offshore, greatly alter the face of this frontier. Before long, however, the sand is returned to the beach by the constant action of the smaller swells.

Beaches can reveal much about the plant and animal life of the sea. Unlike city beaches which are 'groomed' regularly, in more remote areas the evidence of the sea's ecology is washed up and remains on shore. Among the slowly bleaching shells and twisted strands of seaweed are desiccated fish and the armoured, though vacant, shells of crabs and other crustacea.

Beyond the reach of the waves, plants strive to stabilise the frontal dunes. A species of spinifex (*S. hirsutus*) is a common coloniser of

Above: A garden of pigface and *Olearia* species grows among the lichen-stained sandstone of Fitzgerald River
National Park, Western Australia.

Right: Lichen growing on the granite coastline of Torndirrup National Park.

this area along with colourful companions such as sea spurge (*Euphorbia paralais*) and species of succulent pig face.

As the front dunes are stabilised by the plants and gradually become built up, the amount of sand and salt spray reaching the rear dunes decreases. This enables taller shrubs and trees to grow and gradually a humus layer is built up.

However, the large expanses of bare dunes which create such evocative scenes of rippled slopes and glare-filled distances, for all their scenic value, are basically sterile landscapes. The wind whips grains of sand along their faces, over time advancing the whole dune before the prevailing wind direction and preventing vegetation from re-establishing.

Coastlines with geologies originating from ancient volcanic activity often have beaches of rounded stones, which provide many

Above: The Younghusband Peninsula stretches for more than 100 kilometres (over 60 miles) along South Australia's coast.

Right: Towering markers of the former coastline, the Twelve Apostles, near Port Campbell, Victoria, continue to resist erosion.

A rainstorm approaches the Pinnacles, Western Australia.

more niches for lifeforms than the sand variety. Weeds grow among clinging molluscs on the underside of rocks kept continually moist by surging waves. Crabs have numerous hiding places and opportunities for scavenging. The stones glint wetly in the sun, their rounded shapes repeated countless times as they describe the arc of the beach.

Many coastal areas alternate beaches with headlands; gentle crescents between rocky outcrops jutting seawards. The beaches grow over time, fed by the eroding headlands. Frequently, rock platforms composed of rock more resistant to erosion extend

Left: White-faced heron, Central Coast, New South Wales.

Opposite page: Reef herons, Bouddi National Park, New South Wales.

Right: A feeding party of royal spoonbills glide through the shallows of Botany Bay, New South Wales. Feeding as a group helps disturb and dislodge the spoonbills' prey of crustacea and worms.

outwards. By absorbing some of the waves' energy before they reach the cliff face, erosion here is also slowed.

Life on these rock platforms is a struggle — there is alternately the danger for plants and animals of drying out at low tide, and the threat of being swept away by waves at other times. The seaweeds and molluscs which do survive here grow in areas where water coverage is more constant, and have developed very strong holdfasts and sucker-like grips for attaching themselves to the rock surface. Crabs' flat bodies and mobility enable them to seek shelter in crannies.

Oystercatchers and turnstones are also found in this zone. These birds are wave wise. They time their foray onto the rock platform as the wave retreats, hurriedly probe among the molluscs, secure a prize, and sprint back to safety as the next wave boils forward.

Often coastal regions create their own weather. The meeting of warm oceans and cool landmasses or vice versa forms clouds, mists, local storms and squalls under the right conditions.

Slabs of sandstone dominate the beaches of Fitzgerald River National Park.

However, wind is the primary force in the coastal environment — rarely is it absent. It builds in strength during the day, forming the wind chop which hurries shoreward from beyond the horizon. The strongest winds originate from the ocean, sweeping in, uninterrupted by landform, to buffet the shore. Nowhere is the wind's form and substance revealed more clearly than in the flight

Island Rock, part of a stratum of 400 million-year-old sandstone in Kalbarri National Park, Western Australia, has proved more resistant to the battery of the Indian Ocean than the rest of the cliff line. Above the sandstone, a stratum of limestone crumbles, forming slopes of rubble on which vegetation struggles to maintain a foothold.

Above: A carpet of *Posidonia* seaweed dries in the sun at Shark Bay in Western Australia. Extensive beds of the seaweed
support many marine creatures, including the dugong.

Right: Yardie Creek, Cape Range National Park, Western Australia.

of the ocean birds. They define its gusts and eddies with small adjustments of their wings, turning parabolas and racing before it, slicing an effortless path into it, or rising high above cliffs on its uplift.

Winds and tumultuous weather, frequent visitors to the coast, play an important role in shaping the nature of light encountered here. The winds are heavy with suspended sea water, picked up from white caps and crashing waves. As light strikes these droplets, it scatters, creating a pearly luminescence and perhaps a small rainbow. Cliff lines and beaches retreat into haze. Offshore winds push the haze away, although a shimmering quality remains as the light reflects cleanly from sand and water.

The weather, and therefore the light, often displays a recurrent nature. Squall lines roll in from the ocean, hiding the sun and dumping rain, only to pass over and allow the sun to reappear. Only the sun's angle changes as the whole day's rhythm is played out this way.

Following page: **This trestle bridge in East Gippsland, Victoria, was built in the early years of this century to carry locomotives across a low-lying area. Maintenance workers received extra 'height' money when manoeuvring new beams into place.**

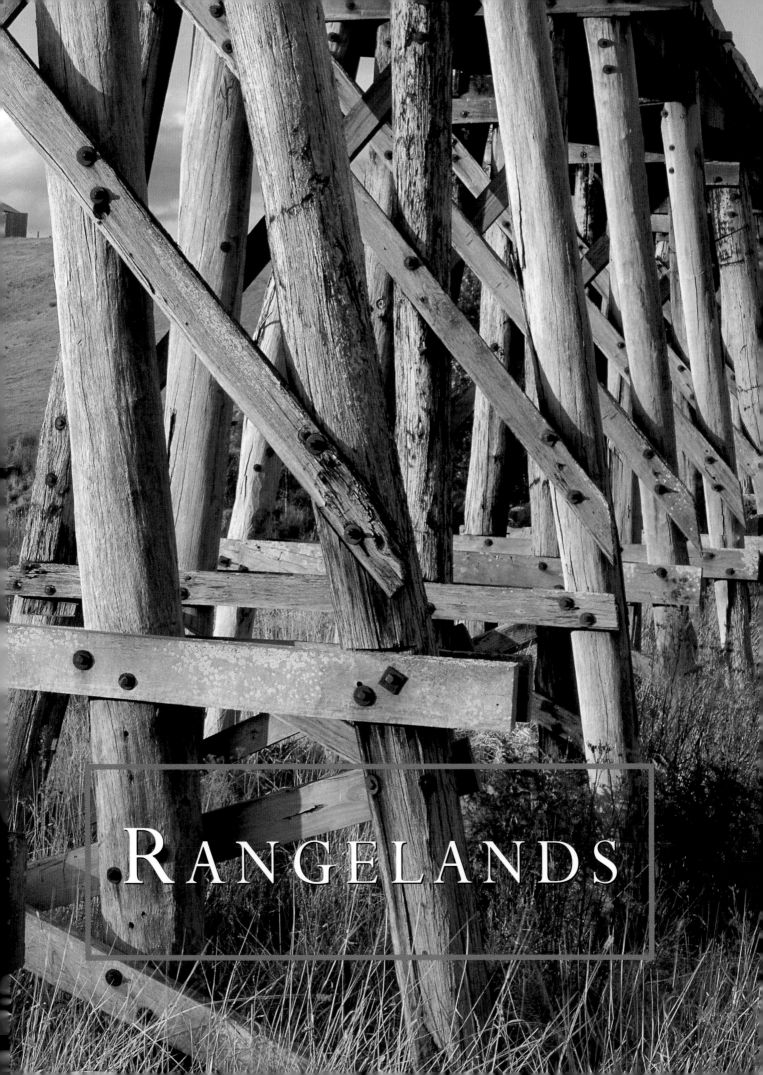

RANGELANDS

THE GREAT DIVIDE EXTENDS DOWN THE EASTERN SIDE OF THE CONTINENT, FORMING ONE OF THE

LONGEST GEOLOGICAL FEATURES ON EARTH. FROM CAPE York to Victoria the slopes and hills of these rangelands have a remarkable similarity of appearance — grassy hills dotted with eucalypts.

Accounting for this region's largely homogenous appearance are the agricultural pursuits that have long been practised on the ranges. Woodlands and forests have been replaced by pasture for cattle and sheep. The productive, well-watered rangelands were settled early in Australia's European history for this purpose, following on the heels of the explorers who opened up the country.

The proximity of the rangelands to towns and cities means that this type of landscape is viewed by most Australians as 'the country', as distinct from the outback. The rangeland region is familiar picturesque country, well serviced and safe. It is also vast, a fact hidden by the close horizons and only revealed from high vantage points.

Hilltops curve and flow downwards to valleys in rounded steps, creating horizons near and distant — the horizon constantly changes with the viewpoint. The boundary between land and sky is more of a transition, a perception enhanced when round, billowing clouds fill the sky.

The long period of human settlement has greatly contributed to the character of the rangelands — faded, sometimes restored buildings, ranging from the grand, to the most basic constructions of timber and iron, are as much features of the countryside as the

vegetation and topography. Most country towns and villages have wonderful collections of past architectural styles. The classic two or three storey pub, a probably disused picture theatre, spreading verandahs and ragged fencelines combine to create the distinctive character of these areas, a character built up over the decades, and now enhanced by the mark of age.

Some abandoned farmhouses are classics of their kind — tree limb verandah posts, grey warping weatherboard, corrugated iron patches and a skeletal wooden framework showing where timber shingles have fallen away. Sometimes only the brick or stone chimneys stand above weathered debris — bleak reminders of the comfort they once provided to the vanished homesteaders.

Inhabited farmhouses have long since settled on their foundations amid old bushes and venerable trees. Verandahs of curved corrugated iron provide a transition to the outdoors.

Work buildings have a simple rustic elegance. Milking or shearing sheds are placed among pens, fences and gates that contain and guide the livestock. The ground here is usually so

Right:
Constructed of corrugated iron (including the window shades), this cottage near Dimboola, Victoria, sits in the midst of a windswept paddock.

Previous page:
Hillsides raked with sunlight, Wollemi, New South Wales.

Its working days over, a tractor slowly rusts in a paddock near the Turon River in central New South Wales.

trampled that it is either muddy or dusty, depending on the weather, accounting for the ubiquitous gumboots standing in sentry rows near backdoors.

Sheep are packed into the pens at shearing time, their woolly bodies compressing until a solid square of wool and bleating heads is formed. Excited dogs with lolling tongues skim over the living

Following page: **Rain clouds hang over the foothills of the Snowy Mountains, New South Wales.**

Right: **Even the metal on this 1940s truck has been colonised by lichen. I discovered it near Bendoc, Victoria. The dairy farmer who owns the wreck was planning to rid himself of it, but I urged him to keep it in place for atmosphere.**

Left: **Stark dead trees complement the architectural simplicity of this shearing shed near Lake Bolac, Victoria.**

surface like water striders on a pond, occasionally disappearing under the woolly mass and bobbing up elsewhere. Hooves drumming on wooden ramps, yapping and bleating, gates creaking home, whistles and the hum and beat of shearing machinery split

the rural peace, but are as much a part of the countryside as the still of dawn and the carolling of magpies.

On dairy farms cattle trudge to the milking sheds in a sedate and orderly manner, as aware of the routine as the farmers marshalling them. The bustle and manhandling characteristic of the shearing sheds are absent here. The cows slot into the milking spaces, nose into the feed bin, and calmly munch until the milking is completed. The heavy work falls to the farmers, who lug and load the milk cans, and work to keep them, the machinery and the surroundings hygienic. This is a constant job, as cows are not noted for their table manners.

Above: **This now abandoned general store at Hill End, New South Wales, is a relic from the gold-mining boom that swept the area in the early 1870s.**

Left: **Patches of the original woodland environment of the rangelands remain, providing a habitat for native animals, and stabilising the soil.**

A remarkable collection of wooden fences at Hill End, New South Wales.

The tracks on which farmers' four wheel drives or utilities bounce and jolt connect with laneways, in turn giving way to gravel roads which finally reach the highways. This network of roads and tracks gives access to most of the countryside and reveals many of the sights that elude travellers hurrying along the highways.

The roads also create their own scenery. Rain runs off the raised, exposed surfaces and collects in pools on the verges. This creates micro-environments as extensive as the roads are long.

Many flowers grow here, and often the roadside verges are havens for

native species which are rare or lost from the grazed paddocks. These untended gardens form a bright contrast to the dull grey of the asphalt road.

The bridges which span the range country's frequent creeks and rivers are widely varying constructions — they range from the standard rattling timber example to the large steel and wood 'Meccano sets' spanning the wider rivers. The older bridges have a special architectural charm enhanced by their weathered appearance, and the knowledge of their yeoman service over the decades.

Rivers and creeks form a ribbon of life distinct from the surrounding countryside. Great shoals of sand and pebbles form on river bends, where the sun dancing on broken water fills the surrounds with reflected light. The smaller streams have their own

Constructed of tree limbs and corrugated iron, this hay shed at Cobungra, Victoria, is typical of practical bush architecture, utilising materials from the immediate environment.

character. Cloaked by the limbs of willows, or stands of river red gum, they are, where water quality allows, the home of water rat, platypus and native fish such as golden perch, yellowbelly and Murray cod. The river valleys are hugged by mists which flow down from the hilltops to form a last stand against the heat of the rising sun.

Hillsides are sculpted by raking sunlight. For much of the day the hills present an obtuse angle to the sun, and the texture of the grasses, rocks and trees is highlighted. Shadowed on one side, the hills form a muted background to stark dead trees or old farmhouses drenched in sunlight. As the sun shifts, the modelling

78

effect changes as shadows encroach and new areas are lit. The scene continues to re-create itself with the passage of the sun, so that an area can be unrecognisable when visited several hours apart.

The rangelands have been changed and shaped by people so that they differ greatly from their original state. There is still space for those aspects of the natural world that have been able to adapt to, or even benefit from, the changed conditions. Parrots, magpies, birds of prey, marsupials and reptiles exist along with introduced species. Amid the paddocks and farmhouses, wildlife still has its place, adding a touch of continuity to a changed landscape.

Left: Snow-bearing clouds loom over paddocks near Tumut, southern New South Wales, in early spring. The stream will soon swell with melted snow from higher peaks.

Right: Grazing country extends to the foot of the Flinders Ranges, South Australia.

Following page: Silverton, New South Wales.

PLAINS

AS YOU TRAVEL
FURTHER INLAND,
THE HILLS OF THE RANGE
COUNTRY BEGIN TO DIMINISH UNTIL THEY
BECOME ONLY MINOR INTERRUPTIONS TO THE HORIZON.
This occurs gradually, but a point usually comes when, climbing a last rise, there spreads before you, seemingly without limit, a vast plain. In camouflage dun, yellow and green, vegetation forms a patchwork across the plain, yielding in places to the uniformity of horticultural paddocks. Trees are smudges floating on the horizon, the only disturbance to the flatness.

Two perceptions alter upon entering the plains country. One concerns the sense of progress, of distance travelled. The lack of variation in the landscape means there is little by which to judge progress — it seems as if the horizon merely retreats. The drone of the car engine and the rushing past of the road verges make the experience rather like being on a treadmill.

The other illusion concerns the sky. The flat landscape seems to draw the sky towards it. The sky becomes a vast bowl, and the only apparent boundary to the extent of the countryside.

Because of the sense of space, the plains can be exhilarating places. Uninterrupted fields of golden wheat ripple in waves, spread out beneath billowing clouds that are massive, though insubstantial, stand-ins for mountains and valleys. The linear feel of the plains is emphasised by diminishing fences and converging railway lines.

Light reflects from the languid flow of the big rivers. While the tributaries of the main waterways are often dry (although well studded with river red gums), the larger rivers form wide, brown expanses — the only major variation in the plains' topographic uniformity.

A weathered FJ Holden, west of Broken Hill, New South Wales.

Above: **An outbuilding gradually yields to the elements near Quorn, South Australia.**

Right: **A majestic river red gum near Hawker, South Australia.**

In the absence of prominent landforms, the structures of settlement are the most obvious things to be seen. Those icons of the rural scene, windmills, are conspicuous, performing their task of pumping water from underground bores into troughs and dams with creaking complaint. In cattle and sheep regions, hooves constantly trample the ground at these watering points, ensuring a dusty circle surrounds them. Trails leading away from the water are marked by a plume of dust rising behind the straggling mobs.

Windmills are also a focus for great flocks of cockatoos, which congregate, chattering and disputing. When disturbed, they explode raucously into the air, manoeuvring as one. The birds'

aerial acrobatics, impressive as they are, don't always enable them to avoid an oncoming car. (Kangaroos have a similar tendency for hazardous behaviour. While content to graze during the day and watch cars go by without interest, at night headlights seem to inspire them to lunge in the direction of the moving car. Driving at night on the plains can cause more stress than it is worth.)

Among the most impressive of the human structures on the plains are the great shearing sheds. Taking full advantage of the level ground, they sometimes spread over 50 metres (yards). They rest, like inland wharves, on numerous wooden posts which firmly plant the structure on the ground.

Shearing sheds capture an essence of Australia that resists the passage of time. Their long-established design creates an extremely functional work building. The pens, entry and exit ramps, wool bins, classing tables, pulley machines and presses need only flexible backs and buzzing shears to keep the operation running smoothly. The broad timber floorboards are kept preserved by the lanolin from the sheep's backs — the sheep inadvertently polish them

Previous page: This racetrack near Wilcannia, New South Wales, has rather spartan facilities. The track is either good or impassable.

Left: **Correllas explode into the air, Kimberley region, Northern Territory.**

Opposite page: **Clouds move swiftly over a blue-bush-dotted plain near Mootwingee, New South Wales.**

whilst being dragged to the shears. Many presses proclaim the name of their nineteenth century manufacturer in florid script, even as they continue to perform perfectly. In appearance and function the shearing sheds link Australia with its pioneering days.

Ruins also dot the plains. Most of them are a testament to the marginal and inconsistent rainfall of the region. Superseded work buildings and yards, or the remains of old homesteads — the weather causes them to deteriorate equally. Stone walls crumble, boards warp and twist, and iron stains red.

Some structures are abandoned most of the year, but can come to life suddenly and dramatically. The bush racetracks and showgrounds usually stand deserted and cheerless amid whipping dust and creaking iron, the haunts of crows. However, two or three times a year they may play host to a rodeo or race meet, and colour and movement briefly displace the desolation. They are basic constructions — a dusty track or ring, iron fences, tin sheds and corrugated iron dunnies; but among the hats, bare-footed children, steak sandwiches and beer, is the flash of brown shanks and glamorous sheen of silk.

Only clouds interrupt the strong flow of light onto the plains. On roofs, outbuildings and water tanks, the hard lines of corrugated iron form rows of light and shadow. Without significant landform to block sunlight, the rays of a low sun race

Previous page: **An enormous woolshed near Nyngan, New South Wales.**

Above: **A collection of old lamps and bottles in an abandoned store, central New South Wales.**

Right: **The beginnings of the plains, Horsham, Victoria.**

across the landscape. It seems to barely catch on the grass, and only trees, hay ricks and farm buildings provide some resistance to its rush. The setting sun also contributes to the sense of distance on the plains, as the sun dips to the far horizon, briefly linking land and sky.

Following page: Karri trees compete for light and space in Shannon National Park, Western Australia.

Left: Dry raddle for marking sheep and a vintage weighing machine are some of the tools of the shearing trade.

Opposite page: A small shearing shed near Ningaloo, Western Australia. A wooden press, classing tables, wicker baskets and lanolin-stained floorboards are typical features.

FORESTS

AUSTRALIA HAS A WIDE RANGE OF FOREST TYPES, FROM THE MOUNTAIN ASH FORESTS OF VICTORIA AND

TASMANIA TO THE TROPICAL RAINFORESTS OF NORTHERN Queensland. However, all forests share a common theme — they are, by their nature, closed worlds, with a tranquility and internal order that sets them apart from other natural environments.

There are both broad and subtle differences between the ecologies of different types of forest. These are based on species composition, soil type, climate and degree of canopy cover. However, in all types of forest the role of the canopy is critical.

The most important role of the canopy is as a photosynthesis factory. In this process chlorophyll in the tree's leaves captures the light energy of the sun and, in conjunction with water and atmospheric carbon dioxide, enables the tree to form starch and glucose. This energy store powers the growth of the tree. The canopy also acts as a water pump. As the sun evaporates water molecules from the leaf's surface, the next molecule is drawn upwards by cohesive bonding. This process extends through narrow xylem vessels all the way to the tip of the roots, each molecule moving upwards in turn. A large tree can pump into the atmosphere hundreds of litres (gallons) of water a day.

While the solar-powered canopy drives the forest, at ground level other vital activity occurs. A constant rain of leaf and bark debris decays into humus through the action of bacteria and insects. The humus then returns nutrients to the trees and shrubs.

Eucalypt species form 95 per cent of Australia's forests. Outstanding examples of eucalypt forests are found at opposite ends of the continent. The karri forests of Western Australia and

the mountain ash, blue gum and shining gum forests of southern New South Wales, Victoria and Tasmania, are all characterised by stands of tall trees, spacious interiors and relatively open canopies. A healthy growth of smaller trees, shrubs and ferns is due to the generous amount of light which penetrates the canopy.

Karris share the south-west region with smaller-sized jarrah, marri, blackbutt and peppermint (among others); the distribution of species is dependent on soil, aspect, topography and climate. These forests end abruptly where extruding granite forms open areas colonised by moisture-loving plants.

The make-up of species in the forests of the south-east of the continent also reflects the immediate environment. Topography for example, can influence rainfall and evaporation while temperature (a 6 degree Celsius (10.8 degree Fahrenheit) difference for every 1000 metres (yards) ascended) also favours certain species. Harsher conditions can result in stands of a single species that is best adapted.

Eucalypts evolved in response to a loss of nutrients in Australia's

Previous page: **Brilliantly coloured sap exudes from this Sydney red gum** *(Angophora costata)* **after heavy rain, Royal National Park, New South Wales.**

Left: **The understorey of this forest near the Stirling Ranges of Western Australia is a colourful medley of pink** *Isopogons*, **orange pea flowers, yellow dryandras and scarlet banksias. Isolated from related species in eastern Australia by the arid regions, the flora of the south-west has evolved into an array of diverse and spectacular species.**

Fertile soil and frequent rainfall provide fuel for the growth of these karri trees *(Eucalyptus diversicolor)* in Western Australia. Some reach 85 metres (280 feet) in height. The trees' very specific requirements restrict their habitat to a relatively small region between Albany and Cape Leeuwin.

ancient soils and a gradual drying of the climate. They first appeared 45 million years ago — fossilised pollen has been dated to this period — a time when rainforest covered most of the continent. Eucalypts have become spectacularly successful since that time with over 500 species found in virtually every climatic

Right: **This stream, barely an inch deep, flows over a granite bed in Shannon National Park, Western Australia. The surrounding forest ends abruptly at the edge of the granite outcrop. Mosses, trigger plants, red insectivorous sundews and bladderworts have colonised the granite, sustained by water gradually percolating from the rock.**

Left: **A spider methodically constructs its web in this sub-tropical rainforest in the Illawarra region of New South Wales.**

Following page: **Boulders carpeted with moss, Messmate Forest, Mt Buffalo National Park, Victoria.**

region of Australia. This reflects their adaptability to many environments and ability to benefit from fire. In many species fire is necessary to open the seed capsule, which falls onto the ash-enriched forest floor. A drying climate and increased fire frequency led to the retreat of the rainforests and the rise of the eucalypts

Above: Blechnum water ferns growing from a mossy sandstone wall in Morton National Park, New South Wales.

Right: **New leaf growth, Shannon National Park.**

and other genera. If fire occurs too frequently, eucalypts will colonise a former rainforest area. If, however, there is no recurrence of fire, the swiftly-growing eucalypts help regenerate the rainforest, providing shade for the regrowth of rainforest species.

Rainforests have slowly retreated to their current refuges on ranges and moist tropical areas, but they continue to display all the grandeur of their continent-spanning ancestors. Although there are a number of types of rainforest they share certain aspects in common. The canopy is dense, forming virtually a complete cover. Younger trees stand dormant until an old tree falls. The sunlight

106

pouring through the gap provides the energy for the tree to grow rapidly and fill the space.

The forest floor is relatively free of undergrowth, being composed of small ferns, saplings and tree ferns. The biggest obstacles are the fallen trees, covered by their carpets of moss and fungi. Epiphytic ferns and orchids occupy the middle ground between floor and canopy, clinging to trunks and tree limbs.

Left: **Angophora forest, Ku-ring-gai National Park, New South Wales.**

Below: **Spotted gum and** *Macrozamia* **palm, Mimosa Rocks National Park, New South Wales.**

The complex, species-rich tropical rainforest is, paradoxically, a scene of riotous order. Order is imposed by the shared struggle of plants towards the available light. Myriad leaf shapes brush against the sky, backlit and silhouetted. Most of them are broad and dark green to take full advantage of the light. Vines loop overhead like languid snakes coiled around branches. The trees stretch upward to the sun, firmly anchored by enormous buttressed roots.

Sub-tropical rainforests (noted for their smaller leaf size) and the cool temperate rainforests have a more limited range of species. Humidity, light intensities and the lack of wide temperature changes, however, are common to these rainforests because of the mod-ifying influence of the canopy.

In cool temperate rainforests it is common for stands to be domi-nated by single tree species such as southern sassafras or myrtle beech, growing among tree fern groves of similar ancient lineage. Time's flow is stalled in these magical forests — little has changed since pre-historic times.

109

Perceptions change upon entering a forest. You are immediately enclosed within the environment; sight is limited by the density of the trees. At most you may see 300 metres (yards), a radius that bounds perception of the forest, regardless of its size. A visitor moves slowly along the forest floor, eyes drawn upwards by the vertical lines of tree trunks, and glimpses of the sky beyond. Wind is muted and is often noted only by the rustling of innumerable leaves overhead.

Light is also subdued — this is most marked in rainforests. The sunlight that is not intercepted by the rainforest's canopy forms dappled pools of light on the leafy forest floor. Ferns, fungi and mossy logs are briefly lit as the sun angles overhead, raking the sides of trees. So narrow are the beams, they move perceptibly. Leaves and fronds glow like stained glass as, backlit, they reveal their hidden colour.

The novel plays of light are not so pronounced in an open forest. Here there is a sense of airiness and an intermingling of shifting light and shade.

What the eucalypt forests and rainforests have in common is their scarcity in relation to Australia's land mass. The vast arid regions and deforested ranges put into perspective how rare these special environments are, and the responsibility we have to properly protect those that remain.

HIGHLANDS

PARTS OF THE GREAT DIVIDING RANGE DIFFER DRAMATICALLY

FROM THE GENTLY ROLLING COUNTRYSIDE FOUND ALONG MOST OF ITS LENGTH. IN THE HIGH COUNTRY, altitude, topography and geology have combined to create landforms of singular aspect and grandeur.

The common factor of altitude results in similar environmental stresses acting on these regions. While the ecologies may differ according to soil and other natural variations, the constant exposure to extremes of weather produces landforms that are either very rugged, or highly eroded, with coverings of tenacious vegetation.

The highlands are concentrated in an arc that crosses the New South Wales border and continues across north-eastern Victoria. Covered for months by depths of snow, the alps have a rhythm of life that is attuned to extremes. Snow may also briefly touch the perpendicular sandstone highlands of the Blue Mountains west of Sydney, and the superb granite country that extends northwards from the New England district of New South Wales.

The geology of the highest regions of Australia is varied. Some rocks were formed from sediment in large freshwater lakes, others in deep ocean waters, and some by explosive volcanic activity. High peaks such as Mounts Bogong, Feathertop and Hotham are found alongside uplifted plateaus such as Mount Buffalo.

The Kosciusko region, the highest point in Australia, is another plateau. It was shaped by erosive forces into its present relatively gentle profile before it was elevated, along with the rest of the Great Divide, by a rift in the sea floor east of Australia. The rock strata forms a huge block with an eastern tilt and a plunging west-

ern escarpment. In few places of the Kosciusko highlands is it exposed — most is hidden under a deep accumulation of soil. This also reflects the age of the plateau.

Apart from the cold, the alps are regularly swept by winds that often reach gale force. Away from protected valleys, vegetation is low and compact, huddling together or hiding in the lee of boulders. Among the grasses are herbs and heaths, often with heat-conserving waxy or hairy foliage.

In the most exposed areas, the landscape takes on a very rugged character. The rocks are rough and coarse, tree trunks and limbs bend and twist as if seeking shelter behind each other, and stubborn shrubs and lichen cling among barren rocks and thin soil.

Snow gums are the only trees to hold out against the cold of the higher reaches, leaving behind the stands of alpine ash with which they cohabit at lesser altitudes. The snow gums become more gnarled and stunted to-wards the tree line limit of about 1 800 metres (5 900 feet), and develop a multi-stemmed shape, better able to cope with wind and snow.

For the echidna and mountain pygmy possum, the snow provides insulation against even colder air temperatures. The pygmy possum stays active throughout winter, tunnelling under the snow in search of plants and insects. Echidnas — remarkably

Above: **Mist and cloud swirl around the rocky battle-ments of the Jamison Valley in the Blue Mountains, New South Wales.**

Previous page: **Granite tors are stacked like loaves of bread in Cathedral Rock National Park, New South Wales.**

Above: An echidna emerges from one of its staggered winter hibernations to forage for ants.

Following page: Spears of crystallised snow grass are held suspended in
frozen Lake Catani, Mt Buffalo National Park.

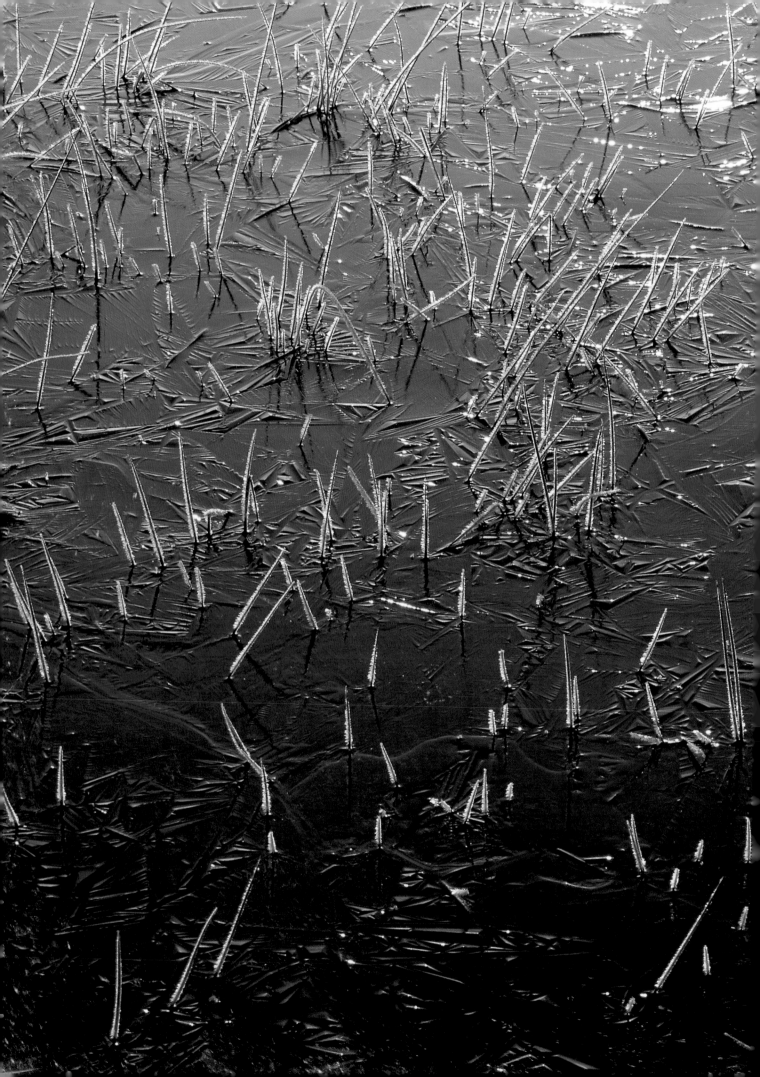

Left: **Heavy weather closes in on the peaks, ridges and valleys of Mount Hotham National Park, Victoria. Snow gums cling to the steep sides of ridges.**

Below: **Milkmaids grow in the shelter of boulders in Girraween National Park, Queensland, taking advantage of water run off.**

versatile animals also found in deserts — are able to remain in the region during winter by hibernating for fortnightly periods, after which their body temperature rapidly rises. They dig free of the snow and trundle off in search of ants to rebuild their energy reserves. The winter passes for them in a series of extended stop-starts. Snakes and skinks 'chill out', hibernating until the spring thaw.

The gradual ascent of most of Australia's highlands disguises the heights that are eventually reached. In the Blue Mountains west of Sydney, however, the altitude is revealed in sudden and dramatic fashion. In a series of magnificently eroded plateaus, great faces of sandstone rise above thickly forested valleys blue with haze from eucalyptus oil vapour. The escarpments and ramparts form extended vistas, following rivers and tributaries that have helped carve out the

Above: This smooth wall of sandstone overlooking the Jamison Valley in the Blue Mountains, owes its clean, relatively unweathered appearance to the fact that a huge mass of stone broke away from the cliff edge in 1931.

Right: Pillars of granite form The Cathedral, Mount Buffalo National Park.

monumental valleys. The great distances and heights are sensed before seen, in the hush of open space spreading out from the valleys to encompass the ridgetops and forested plateaus.

The sandstone of which these highlands are predominantly formed was deposited by rivers over a period of 50 million years beginning 280 million years ago. At times the deposition occurred under the sea and lakes; the source and mode varied greatly over time, accounting for the varied sandstones, shales and coal deposits found in the mountains today.

The erosion of the sandstone has created superb landforms. While minor weathering of the rock surface occurs constantly, weathering within cracks and on underlying softer strata leads to the shearing off of great blocks of stone, clearing a calamitous path to the valley floor, and leaving behind the impressive starkness of

Above: **The Eucumbene River meanders through Kiandra Valley, Kosciusko National Park, New South Wales, swollen with the melted snow of spring. Snow grass emerges unaffected by months under the snow.**

Right: **Three Mile Creek, Kosciusko National Park.**

Above: The sinuous, twisting trunks of snow gums, Kosciusko National Park.

Following page: Granite tors rest in a delicate balancing act in Girraween National Park, Queensland.

the rock face. Dramatic vistas in the Blue Mountains, Wollemi and Kanangra-Boyd areas illustrate the incredible amount of material that has eroded in this relentless, and occasionally catastrophic, fashion. It is also slow — the cliffs retreat less than 200 metres (yards) per 1 million years.

Caves and overhangs sculpted by blown sand and also, from

Left: The coarse texture of the granite Woolpack Rocks in Cathedral Rock National Park is due to the extremes of temperature in this environment. Temperatures can swing from freezing point, to 40 degrees Celsius (100 degrees Fahrenheit) in summer.

Right: An underground stream has polished this granite to a smooth, reflective finish in Girraween National Park.

within, by percolating water (which frees binding iron and clay particles), are also distinctive features of sandstone. The eroding wind soughs musically through the chasms and hollows.

Compared to the densely vegetated valleys, the ridges feature

Above: The Grampians, Victoria, rise in ancient grandeur above the surrounding plains. The mountains form the southern most tip of the Great Dividing Range.

Right: A wedge-tailed eagle rides an uplift air current in Bald Rock National Park, New South Wales.

sparser, smaller trees rising above an understorey of acacias, grevilleas, hakeas and other heath vegetation. The thinner soil, greater exposure to wind and cold, and higher evaporation rates combine to inhibit growth. At the point where a precipice seems to leap into space, the hardiest and most opportunistic plants are found. Cliff mallee ash find niches on the vertical walls, while hanging ferns and grasses are fed by waterfall spray and percolation.

The rock base of the Great Divide also breaks through to create striking terrain in the granite country of northern New South Wales and Queensland. Large tracts of exposed rock loom above wooded valleys, and great tors of granite rest on platforms and ledges, finely balanced like the playthings of giants. There is another powerful expression of the carving force of the elements in a series of block-like towers found in Cathedral Rock National Park, New South Wales — a rugged terrain of stacked granite cubes that both inspires and inhibits approach.

Water run-off from the exposed rock results in local tall forests around the base of the monoliths, and swampy areas that are

havens for fish and frogs. Streams cut through the granite in places, disappearing underground and polishing channels through the rock.

Two hundred million years ago the rock of the granite belt was a molten mass deep within the earth. As it rose and cooled, cracks developed, some of which were filled by rushes of molten rock to create the dykes found today. The sedimentary rock above the granite was slowly worn away, and stress cracks developed as the weight above lessened. Combined with the earlier cracking from cooling, the granite was left in block form. Spectacular tors were formed by a process of exfoliating or onion skin weathering.

Australia's high country is subject to sudden changes of weather. Clouds form readily as cool, moist air rises, and the sun is often hidden from view. Frequent rain clears the air of haze, and when the sun pierces the clouds, the light is invariably strong and clear. Often low cloud envelopes the landscape, muting colours into a wash of grey and green.

Above: **Bald Rock National Park.**

Right: **Sunset, Mt Buffalo National Park, Victoria.**

The span of time in which natural forces have worked in concert to produce the landscape of the high country, and, indeed the rest of Australia, has little meaning from a human perspective. Our best grasp of the concept is found in the wild beauty of the landscape's evolving spectacle, in which the sculpting hand of time and the elements underlies all.